MONSTER MADNESS

Other books by Jack Stokes:
MIND YOUR A'S AND Q'S
LOONY LIMERICKS
107¾ ELEPHANT JOKES

Monster Madness

Outrageous Jokes About Some Weird Folks

Written and illustrated by **Jack Stokes**
Doubleday & Company, Inc.
Garden City, New York

Library of Congress Cataloging in Publication Data

Stokes, Jack.
  Monster madness.

  SUMMARY: An illustrated collection of monster jokes, puns,
and limericks.
  1. Monsters—Anecdotes facetiae, satire, etc.
2. Wit and humor, Juvenile. [1. Jokes. 2. Mon-
sters—Anecdotes, facetiae, satire, etc.] I. Title.
PN6231.M665S7   818′.5407
Library of Congress Catalog Card Number 80–2068
ISBN: 0-385-15690-1 Trade
ISBN: 0-385-15691-x Prebound
Copyright © 1981 by Jack Stokes

To my mummy

How do you know if a monster likes you?
He takes another bite.

What do you get if you cross the bride of
    Frankenstein with a warlock?
Who cares?

DRACULA: Do you love me?
VAMPIRA: *You're a pain in the neck.*

What is the first safety rule for witches?
Don't fly off the handle.

What do you call a person that isn't afraid of
    vampires?
The late . . .

FRANKENSTEIN: What do you do when you hear
    the police coming?
DR. JEKYLL: *Hyde!*

A tremendous gorilla was King Kong.
He liked to hear bells going ding dong!
   But when he shook a steeple,
   It scared all the people,
As there isn't much tune when they ring wrong.

POLTERGEIST: Knock! Knock!
GHOST: *Whoo's there?*

Why doesn't the Abominable Snowman ever
   attack anyone?
He has cold feet.

What do you get if you cross a vampire with your
   mother-in-law?
A hickey that won't go away.

QUASIMODO: I hope my hunch is right.
DRACULA: *Let's prey.*

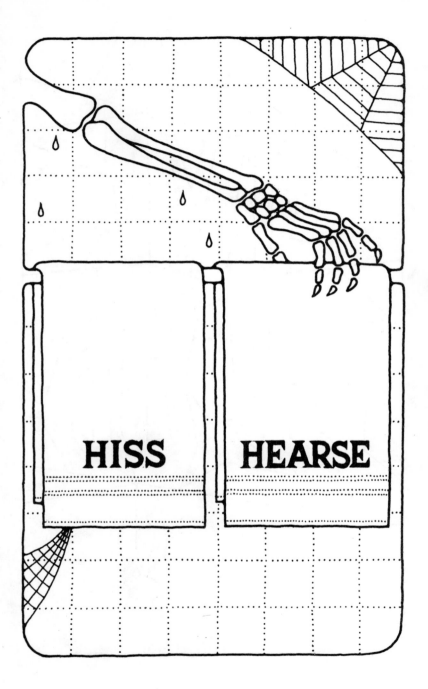

How can you tell a zombie from a bureaucrat?
You can't.

THING: I have to hand it to you.
WITCH DOCTOR: *I always try to do the rite, Thing.*

What do you call a sick monster?
You can try calling him a doctor—if you know one that will come.

What happens when you cross Lon Chaney with a bowling champion?
The phantom strikes again!

What should you do for a vampire bite?
Are you sure you really want one?

PRISONER: This strikes me as strange.
IRON MAIDEN: *You'll get the point!*

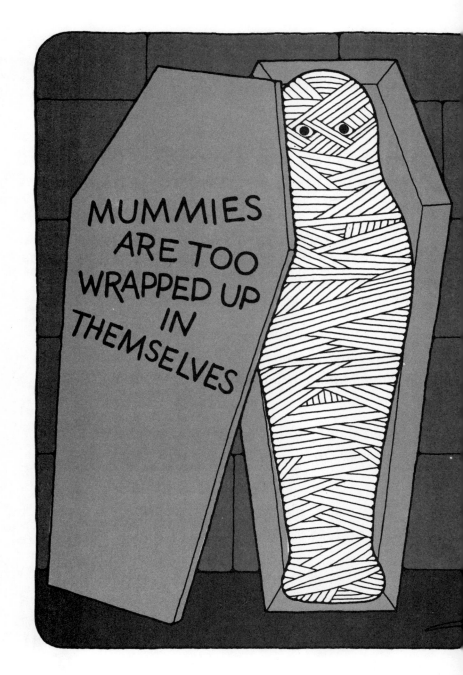

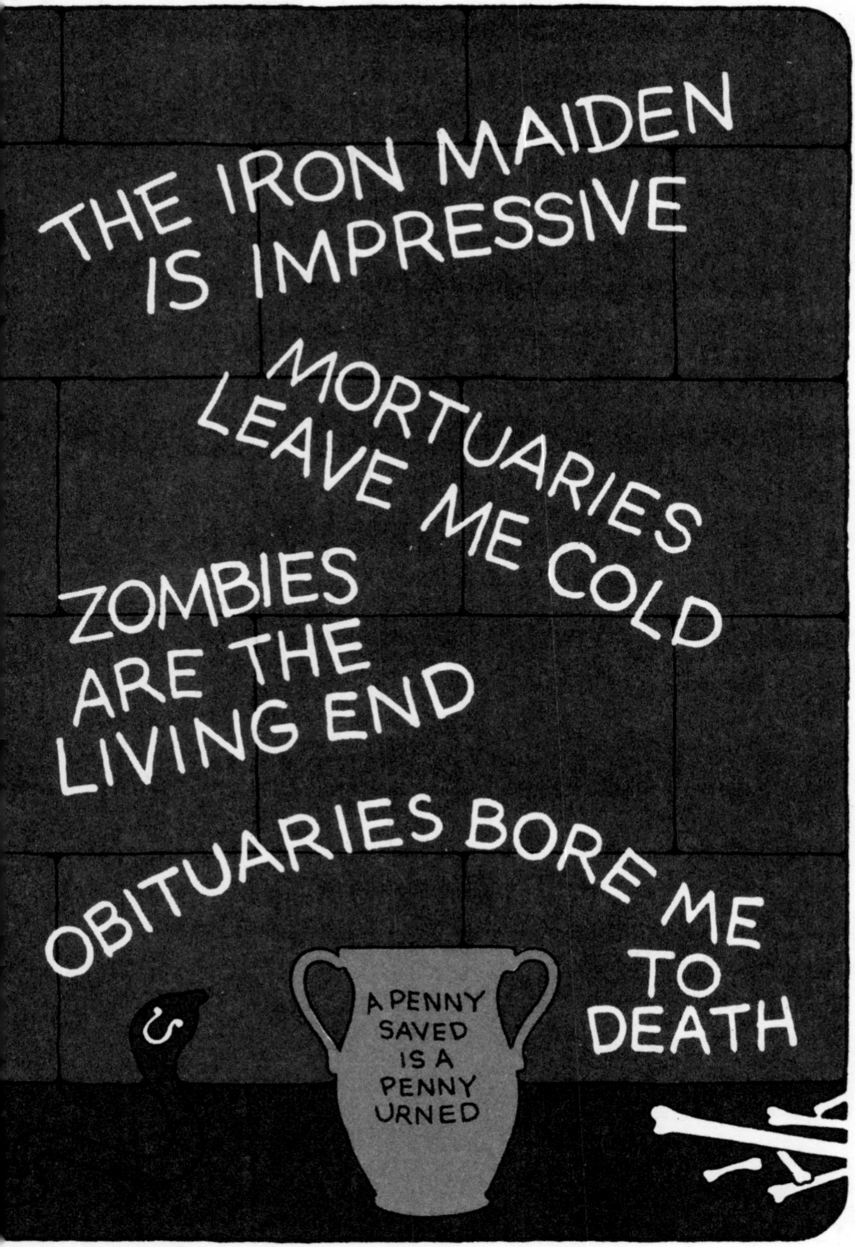
THE IRON MAIDEN IS IMPRESSIVE
MORTUARIES LEAVE ME COLD
ZOMBIES ARE THE LIVING END
OBITUARIES BORE ME TO DEATH
A PENNY SAVED IS A PENNY URNED

Frankenstein had a young bride
Whose cooking he could not abide.
  He tried to explain
  But she hadn't a brain
And her eyeballs fell out when she cried.

What does a vampire get an hour?
About two and a half pints.

Why doesn't anyone ever catch the Loch Ness
  Monster?
Maybe they do but don't recognize the symptoms.

MEDUSA: Look at me!
CYCLOPS: *Eye am.*

What ever happened to the Cabinet of Dr.
  Caligari?
They all resigned.

14

MARLEY: I knew a ghostwriter once.
SCROOGE: *How in the Dickens did you meet him?*

Where do ghosts go on vacation?
Lake Erie.

IGOR: Who do you think you are anyway?
FRANKENSTEIN'S MONSTER: *Henry, George, Bob, Ralph, Al . . .*

A wicked old witch from the West
Used to work evil spells with some zest.
   But if you ever caught her
   And splashed her with water
There'd be nothing left to arrest.

BOSTON STRANGLER: You're a cutup.
JACK THE RIPPER: *You choke me up.*

When are you likely to see monsters?
When you bring home your report card.

"I haven't seen you in a long time."

A FRIENDLY CARD GAME AMONG FIENDS

HENRY VIII: Are there any more Queens?

GIANT: I've got a Jack I don't want.

CYCLOPS: Why can't I ever get two of a kind?

THING: Stop looking at my hand.

IRON MAIDEN: I need a grand slam.

DRACULA: How many points do you have?

FRANKENSTEIN'S MONSTER: Why am I always dummy?

EDGAR ALLAN POE: That's book.

ICHABOD CRANE: Who's a head?

WEREWOLF: We need a new pack.

IGOR: It's my shuffle.

JACK THE RIPPER: I'll cut!

GHOUL: One spade.

KING KONG: What's wild?

WITCH: Let's double the pot.

POLTERGEIST: I'm gonna bump.

DR. VAN HELSING: I like big stakes.

JESSE JAMES: It's my draw.

LIZZIE BORDEN: Let's play Old Maid.

CREATURE FROM THE BLACK LAGOON: Go fish!

HANGMAN: This gallows is a noosence.
CONDEMNED MAN: *Keep your trap shut!*

When would Friday the 13th be really unlucky?
If there were no Saturday the 14th.

What do you get when you cross a werewolf with
   Medusa?
Whatever it is, it will never be a fashion model.

What do you say if you step on a monster's foot?
Help!

What do you get when Dr. Caligari and Dr.
   Frankenstein share an office?
A paradox.

DR. JEKYLL: I've got to change now.
MR. HYDE: That lets me out.
IGOR: There's a switch!

18

QUASIMODO **FOR WHOM THE BELL TOLLS**

DRACULA'S DAUGHTER LIFE WITH FATHER

DR. JEKYLL

HEIDI

IMHOTEP MUMMY DEAREST

THING BOY SCOUT HANDBOOK

JACK THE RIPPER

THE RAZOR'S EDGE

WITCH DOCTOR

VALLEY OF THE DOLLS

KING KONG

WHERE THE WILD THINGS ARE

INVISIBLE MAN

MUCH ADO ABOUT NOTHING

DRACULA

THE GOOD EARTH

BRIDE OF FRANKENSTEIN

LOVE STORY

IMHOTEP: I want my mummy.

Karloff, Lugosi and Chaney
Like nights that are cloudy and rainy.
  They are awfully mean,
  Have Morticia as queen
And think of King Kong as a trainee.

What do you get when you cross a ghost with a
  cow?
Vanishing cream.

DRACULA: Is this a stakeout?
GENIE: *Don't you wish!*

What cheese is appropriate for Halloween parties?
Munster.

What's a good vampire's name?
There aren't any good vampires.

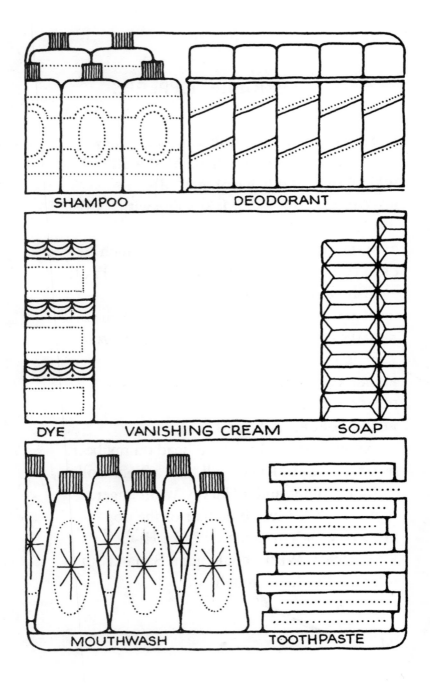

SHAMPOO DEODORANT

DYE VANISHING CREAM SOAP

MOUTHWASH TOOTHPASTE

TERRIBLE TIPPLERS

LADY MACBETH: I'll have a Bloody Mary.

DRACULA: Me too. No, make that a Stinger.

WEREWOLF: I'd like a Scotch Mist.

BOSTON STRANGLER: Make mine with a twist.

WITCH DOCTOR: I want a Zombie.

ZOMBIE: How about a Caribbean Punch?

CREATURE FROM THE BLACK LAGOON: Try the Fish House Punch.

IRON MAIDEN: I make some good punches.

ABOMINABLE SNOWMAN: I'd like a Frozen Daiquiri.

EDGAR ALLAN POE: I'd like Old Crow.

DEMON: Rum.

PETER LORRE: A Sour.

ICHABOD CRANE: Just put a head on my beer.

DRACULA'S DAUGHTER: I'll take a Tom Collins, a John Collins and a Harvey Wallbanger.

WOLFMAN: I need some hair of the dog.

PHANTOM OF THE OPERA: I like Hi-C.

KING KONG: Wish I could get a Banana Split.

LURCH: I've had enough.

"Would you prefer a tailor-made suit
or something off the rack?"

DRACULA'S DAUGHTER: Something's a miss.
BRIDE OF FRANKENSTEIN: *Not me!*

What's an advantage to being a Cyclops?
Your eyes never cross.

What do you get when you cross a vampire with a
    doctor?
More blood tests than ever!

What kind of a TV set does Dracula have?
Transylvania.

What is the most important class for witches?
Spelling.

What do you get if you cross Dracula with
    Sleeping Beauty?
Tired blood.

There was an Egyptian mummy
Who had a voluminous tummy.
    But it wasn't his fault.
    They put food in his vault
And it got his sarcophagus crumby.

Why are werewolves hairy?
If they had feathers, they'd be werehens.

What would happen if you crossed the Addams
    Family with the Munsters?
The neighbors would sell.

Where is the best place to see monsters?
From about half a mile away.

QUASIMODO: Your husband came over for a bite
    last night.
MORTICIA: *You've got bats in your belfry!*

CREATURES' CAUCUS

PHANTOM OF THE OPERA: I'll conduct the meeting.

EXECUTIONER: I bow to the chair.

KING KONG: Who's top banana?

HYDRA: I'm a quorum.

GODZILLA: I nominate Dorian Gray for Vice President.

CYCLOPS: Aye.

HEADLESS HORSEMAN: Nay.

THING: Let's have a show of hands.

VOODOO DOLL: I can pinpoint the problem.

IRON MAIDEN: The case is closed.

WITCH: We should have a clean sweep.

DR. CALIGARI: I want a new Cabinet.

SKELETON: I give my support.

GHOUL: I'm revolting.

HANGMAN: We need a strong platform.

DR. VAN HELSING: Are planks anything like stakes?

DR. FRANKENSTEIN: I like amendments.

DRACULA: I hate the Sunshine Law.

WARLOCK: Be careful. The media is here.

MUMMY: Let's have more red tape.

ZOMBIE: Over my dead body.

INVISIBLE MAN: The chair never recognizes me.

GHOST: Me neither.

LURCH: I move we adjourn.

WITCH: Don't get familiar.
PYEWACKET: *You had no rite to say that.*

What do you get if you cross a voodoo doll with a
  postman?
A witch doctor that makes house calls.

When Dracula turns to a bat,
His visits are not for a chat.
  If he's not held in check,
  He'll put marks on your neck.
And then you will need a cravat.

Why doesn't Frankenstein's Monster wear high
  heels?
Maybe he does when you're not around.

Why do vampires drink blood?
Coffee is so expensive.

"She had her face lifted."

COUTURIER
SEMI-CHIC FASHIONS
by QUASI-MODO

BODY
SHOP
FRANK & STEIN
proprietors

KENNEL
SHOPPE

MR. BASKERVILLE
PROPRIETOR

FURRIER

· JACK L. HYDE prop. ·

VAN HELSING'S
STAKE
HOUSE

BELA'S
BIER
PARLOR

GOOD TO THE
LAST DROP

There once was a skinny old witch
Who wrecked her new broom in a ditch.
   When they pulled them both out
   There were looks full of doubt.
As no one could tell which was which.

ADDAMS FAMILY: You're weird, ugly and
  repulsive.
MUNSTERS: *Don't try to make up.*

What happens when you cross King Kong with a
  black cat?
You'll be lucky if it just crosses *your path.*

What's a good monster movie?
Are there any good monsters?

MRS. ZOMBIE: We're going out tonight. Look alive!
MR. ZOMBIE: *Let's stay home. I'm dead!*

"No! I asked for a *half*back."

MRS. GHOST: I have no image.
MR. GHOST: *That's the spirit!*

What did Rigor Mortis say at the undertaker's
   convention?
"Do you mind if I set in?"

What would you get if you crossed Dr.
   Frankenstein with Dracula?
An acupuncturist.

SPIRITUALIST: What size robe should I get?
CLERK: *You look like a medium.*

Can you tell a vampire from a chicken?
You probably make rotten Tetrazzini if you can't.

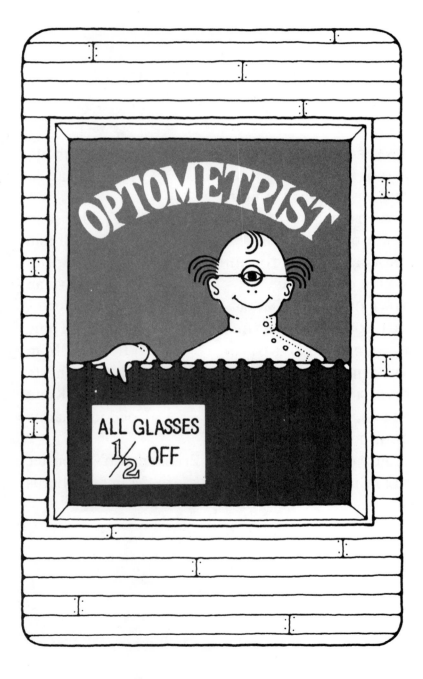

MONSTER MELODIES
(in concert)

JINGLE BELLS	Quasimodo
PEG O' MY HEART	Dracula
GET ME TO THE CHURCH ON TIME	Bride of Frankenstein
CLAIR DE LUNE	Wolfman
ON A SLOW BOAT TO CHINA	Fu Manchu
WHITE CHRISTMAS	Abominable Snowman
THAT OLD BLACK MAGIC	Witch Doctor
PUT YOUR HAND IN THE HAND	Thing
I GOT PLENTY O' NUTTIN'	Invisible Man
ALL THROUGH THE NIGHT	Ghosts
GIVE MY REGARDS TO BROADWAY	King Kong
HELLO, DOLLY!	Voodoo Charms
JOHN BROWN'S BODY and PUT ON A HAPPY FACE	Frankenstein's Monster
BLEST BE THE TIE THAT BINDS	Mummy Chorus

INTERMISSION
(potions will be served in the lobby)

THE LOST CHORD	Boston Strangler
I DON'T WANT TO SET THE WORLD ON FIRE	Dragon
THERE'LL BE A HOT TIME IN THE OLD TOWN TONIGHT	Lucifer
TREES	Werewolves
MY HEART BELONGS TO DADDY	Dracula's Daughter
BE KIND TO YOUR WEB-FOOTED FRIENDS	Creature from the Black Lagoon
SHOO-SHOO BABY	Sasquatch
I'M GONNA WASH THAT MAN RIGHT OUTA MY HAIR	Medusa
ALL OF ME	Skeleton
I LOVE YOU TRULY	Henry VIII
TAPS	Poltergeists

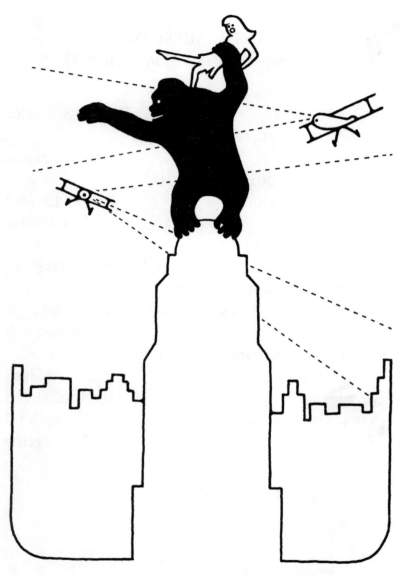

"Okay, I've seen the skyline. Now let's go to Central Park."

VOODOO CHARM: You're the kind of man only a mummy could love.
ZOMBIE: *You're no doll!*

What do you call a place that has lots of Gremlins?
A parking lot.

There once was a Jekyll and Hyde.
Who was who was quite hard to decide.
   That one was so bad
   Made the other one sad,
Till the end, when their fates coincide.

What do you get when you cross Wolfman with a barber?
A conflict of interests.

GHOST: You're a good mixer.
LUCREZIA BORGIA: *I can see through you.*

THE BRIDE OF FRANKENSTEIN
GOT STOOD UP
POLTERGEISTS
LIKE TO KNOCK AROUND
BELA LUGOSI
PLAYED BIT PARTS

A black and quite juicy young spider
Tried drinking some fermented cider.
   With her senses in ebb,
   She fell out of her web.
What a splat with the cider inside her!

What do you get if you cross a ghost with an
   elephant?
A big nothing.

JACK THE GIANT KILLER: You can't spell.
WITCH: *You don't know beans.*

Why are ghosts invisible?
Ask the one sitting next to you.

What do you get if you cross a vampire with a
   rhinoceros?
Whatever it is, thank goodness it sleeps all day.

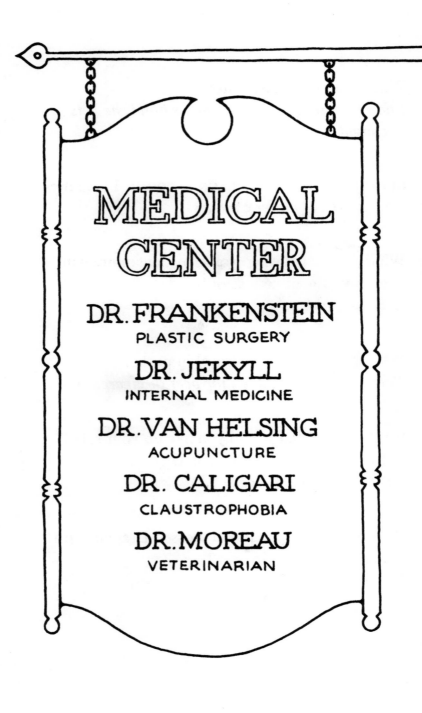

What makes a monster story?
I don't know, but no one spanks him if he gets caught.

CREATURE FROM THE BLACK LAGOON: I love dips.
KING KONG: *I prefer canapés.*

What do you get when you cross a vampire with an investment counselor?
A blood bank.

Why don't werewolves travel in packs?
They might be mistaken for beer or cigarettes.

WAITRESS: What would you like on your salad? Italian? French? Or Russian?
GODZILLA: *One of each.*

What would happen if you crossed Dracula with Frankenstein's Monster?
Nothing, Dracula doesn't like crosses.

"He's been like that since he made Whoo's Whoo!"

DREADFUL DINING

ZOMBIE: I'll take orders now.

DR. VAN HELSING: I'll have a stake.

ICHABOD CRANE: It's probably horsemeat.

MUMMY: Try the dried beef.

WITCH: I'd like the boiled dinner.

ABOMINABLE SNOWMAN: Do you have frozen foods?

DRACULA: I just grab a bite here and there.

MADAME TUSSAUD: Give me wax beans.

GIANT: I hate beans.

BRIDE OF FRANKENSTEIN: I don't care as long as I don't have to cook.

SKELETON: I could use some spareribs.

SASQUATCH: I hope they have pig's feet.

THING: I like finger food.

WARLOCK: Are frog's legs as good as toad's legs?

CREATURE FROM THE BLACK LAGOON: Fish chowder! How gross!

QUASIMODO: I love toll house cookies.

FRANKENSTEIN'S MONSTER: I'd like a little bit of everything.

INVISIBLE MAN: No matter what I eat it doesn't show.

KING KONG: Now, maybe I can get a banana split.

WOLFMAN: May I have a doggie bag?

Why do witches ride broomsticks?
Have you priced cars recently?

SKELETON: No bones about it.
VAMPIRE: *That never dawned on me.*

Count Dracula had a young daughter
Who learned to drink blood and not water.
   When she was at school
   She played it so cool
That none of the teaching staff caught her.

How does a lady vampire put on her makeup if
   she can't see herself in a mirror?
Very badly.

Why don't we have good monster movies
   anymore?
We have. They're called political messages.

"I see Hazel's been re-possessed again."

PAWING THROUGH THE YELLOW PAGES

AIRLINES
Trans Ylvania

BASEBALL EQUIPMENT—BATS
Bela Lugosi

BOATS—RENTAL
Mary Celeste

CHILDREN'S EXCHANGE
Pied Piper

CUTLERY
Jack the Ripper

DENTURES
Fu Manchu

DUNGEONS—CONSTRUCTION
James Mason

ELECTROCUTIONS
Master Charge

FENCES
Lon Chaney

FLOWERS
Jane Withers

GRAVE MARKERS
Rolling Stones

HAIR REMOVAL
Mr. Hyde

INVESTIGATORS
Richard Pryor

JACKS
The Giant Killer
Mr. Palance

KEYS
Loch Ness Monster

KITCHEN CABINETS
Mrs. Caligari

LAUNDRY
The Iron Maiden

LINEN SUPPLY
The Mummy

MOATS
Lloyd Bridges
Farrah Fawcett
Ethel Waters

MOPEDS
Sasquatch

MUFFLERS
The Boston Strangler

NEEDLEPOINT
Voodoo Bazaar

ORPHANAGES
Gingerbread House

OSTEOPATHS
Basil Rathbone
Red Skelton

PARKING GARAGES
Boris Karloff

QUEENS—SURPLUS
Henry VIII

RECYCLING
Frankenstein's Monster

REDUCING AND WEIGHT CONTROL
Gene Hackman

SPOT REMOVAL
Lady Macbeth

TORTURES
Cornelia Otis Skinner

TYPEWRITERS—REPAIR
Arisztid Olt

UNDERTAKERS
John Barrymore

VANES
Dracula

WAGONS
Van Heflin
Van Helsing

X-RAY
Fay

YARNS
Mary Wollstonecraft Shelley
Bram Stoker
H. G. Wells

ZOOS
Dr. Moreau
King Kong
Wolfman

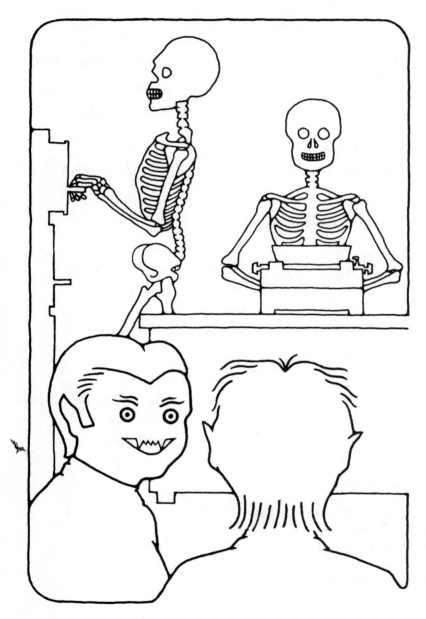

"We're down to a skeleton staff."

Should you try to bite a vampire back?
Not if his neck is convenient.

What do you get if you cross a witch with the
   Creature from the Black Lagoon?
*Whatever it is, it can sure sweep out a pool in a
   hurry.*

A Jr. whose name was Lon Chaney
Liked to make up so scary and zany
   That the ladies would faint.
   But he used water paint
So he had to stay in when 'twas rainy!

LIZZIE BORDEN: I'm only gonna ax you once.
CARDIFF GIANT: *That's big of you.*

Are monsters ever architects?
Who do you think designs parking garages?

What happens when you cross Frankenstein's
   Monster with a frog?
You'll be disappointed when you kiss it.

GHOUL: I dig ya.
CORPSE: *You leave me cold.*

Why did they burn so many witches?
Maybe they had a fuel crisis.

Why aren't some people successful at killing
   vampires?
They make misstakes.

Why don't you see the Invisible Man at Halloween
   parties?
Think about it!

SATAN: You're a dummy!
MADAME TUSSAUD: *How the devil did you know?*

56

MORTICIA: We have a grave situation.
LON CHANEY: *Let's make up.*

There's a legend in old Transylvania
That a count used to have kleptomania.
    As 'twas blood that he took,
    He's a fiend, not a crook.
That's opinion in central Romania.

What do you get if you cross a mummy with a
    stunt man?
A prewrapped patient.

Should you have a rabies shot when a vampire
    bites you?
Don't worry about it. He probably won't even ask.

What do ghosts tell their children?
"You should be heard and not seen."

Do monsters ever take airplanes?
Not if there is something smaller to carry.

What happens if you cross a Ghost with a
Gremlin?
You can never find out why it won't start.

QUASIMODO: I'm back.
GODZILLA: Leapin' Lizards!
KING KONG: You drive me ape!
DRACULA: You drive me batty!
WOLFMAN: That's a howl.
ABOMINABLE SNOWMAN: You're flaky!
FRANKENSTEIN: I'm in stitches.
CREATURE FROM THE BLACK LAGOON: Something's
fishy.

What do you get when you cross a skeleton with a
  teacher?
A quiz you have to bone up for.

LUCREZIA BORGIA: My ol' man is rich.
DRACULA'S DAUGHTER.: *My ol' man will put the
bite on him.*

If you think over there it looks eerie,
To the right or the left makes you leery,
    Then you better stay here;
    Try to live with your fear,
But *don't* look in back of you, dearie!

How did Frankenstein feel about his bride?
Igor!

What do you get when you cross a pine tree with a
  mole?
A casket that buries itself.

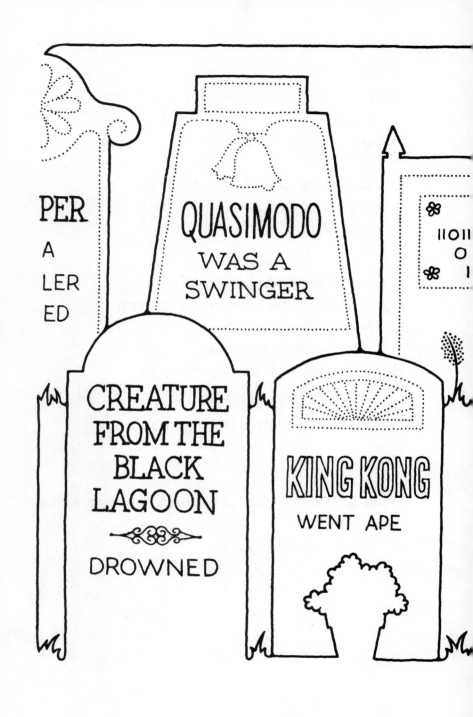